young british muslims
and **relationships**

a Muslim Youth Helpline (MYH) research project
supported by London Councils

Musab Younis

Design and typesetting: Musab Younis
Printing: Ashford Colour Press

ISBN: 978-0-9566461-0-1

Published by
Muslim Youth Helpline
18 Rosemont Road | London | NW3 6NE

Tel: 02074358171
Fax: 08707743519

Website: www.myh.org.uk
Email: info@myh.org.uk

Cover design: Rizwan Hussain and Musab Younis

Cover images, from left to right, by Flickr® users: CharlesFred; Katie Tegtmeyer;
Umm Papoose; Beth Rankin. All licensed under Creative Commons. Some rights
reserved.

Contents

Researcher

Musab Younis

Musab is Research & Advocacy Officer at the Muslim Youth Helpline (MYH). He has a BA in Politics from the University of Nottingham and has worked on research for the Medical Research Council, the Biotechnology and Biological Sciences Research Council, Demos, and the Institute for Government. He is also the Deputy Editor of *Ceasefire*, an independent political and arts magazine.

Advisory Board

Akeela Ahmed

Akeela is the Chief Executive of MYH, which she first joined in January 2009 as Head of Support Services. She has over eight years' experience in providing support to vulnerable individuals both as a front line staff member and as a manager. She has an MSc in Mental Health Studies from the Institute of Psychiatry, Kings College (University of London), and a BSc in Physics from University College (University of London).

Sughra Ahmed

Sughra is a Research Fellow at the Policy Research Centre, Islamic Foundation. Her most recent publication is a national report on young British Muslims, *Seen and Not Heard: Voices of Young British Muslims.* Her current area of research is exploring the migratory and settlement experiences of first-generation Muslims in the UK. She is a trustee of the Interfaith Network UK, and a Director of the Leicester Council of Faiths.

Louise Archer

Louise is Professor of Sociology of Education at King's College (University of London), with a research interest in identities and inequalities of 'race', gender and social class within compulsory and post-compulsory education. She is currently working on a jointly-authored book, *Urban Youth and Education* (Open University Press).

Sultana Choudhury

Sultana is a psychologist and Chartered Scientist. She has a MSc in Health Psychology and a PhD in developmental psychology. She is Principal Lecturer in Psychology and Director of Child, Adolescent and Family Mental Health at the London Metropolitan University, and is also a member of the British Psychological Society. Her latest publication is *Multifaceted Identity of Inter-Ethnic Young People* (Asghate, 2010).

Tufyal Choudhury

Tufayl is a graduate of the Universities of London (SOAS) and Cambridge, and was called to the Bar in 1997 as a member of Inner Temple. He teaches international human rights law at Durham Law School and is a Research Associate at the University of Oxford Centre on Migration, Policy and Society. He is also a senior policy advisor to the Open Society Institute's At Home in Europe Project.

Rokhsana Fiaz OBE

Rokhsana is a founding director of the Change Institute, a research, organisational development and strategic communications consultancy specialising in race, faith and identity. She leads the enterprise's European Network of Experts on Radicalisation (ENER). She received an OBE in 2009 for services to Black and Minority Ethnic communities.

Acknowledgements

The author would like to thank everyone who has supported and participated in this research project, without whom this report would not have been possible.

Rukaiya Jeraj and Akeela Ahmed were very closely involved in the research process at all stages. Thanks also to Milad Ahmed, Samiya Rashid and Iman Said for invaluable assistance, as well as to the shift leaders and many volunteers at MYH who gave their time and unique perspectives.

Sughra Ahmed, Louise Archer, Sultana Choudhury, Tufyal Choudhury, and Rokhsana Fiaz all contributed expert advice and insight as members of the advisory board for this research. Special thanks to Sughra Ahmed for her additional, and exemplary, input and guidance. Mehreen Khan and Kaisari Mirza both ably assisted with the literature review while volunteering at MYH.

Thank you to the team at London Councils, for recognising the importance of this research and generously supporting us throughout the process.

Finally, a particular thanks must be extended to all of those who gave time to be interviewed for this report.

About MYH

The Muslim Youth Helpline (MYH) is a registered, award-winning charity which provides pioneering faith and culturally sensitive services to Muslim youth in the UK.

Our core service is a free and confidential emotional support service available nationally via the telephone, email, internet and through the post. The service uses male and female volunteers trained in active listening skills, all between the ages of 18 and 30 years, to respond to client enquiries.

As well as a dedicated helpline, MYH runs a youth advocacy service based around a website (muslimyouth.net). Our aim is to encourage British Muslim youth to develop peer-support networks, access specialist and mainstream support services, and care for their social and mental well-being. We also run creative projects with diverse groups of young people in London.

Foreword

'Most scientific laws are of this sort: not assiduous reports of detailed data but sweeping Procrustean simplifications.'

Nelson Goodman, *Ways of World Making* (Kleinman 1988)

Until recently, Nelson Goodman's observation accurately characterised the state of scientific research around ethnic minorities and mental health. Oversimplifications were made; vastly differing groups of peoples were labelled as either 'Black,' 'White' or 'Asian'; their behaviours and modes of living reduced to incorrect stereotypes. Ethnic minority groups including faith groups have consistently been viewed homogenously as 'The Other', and in this capacity scrutinised and dehumanised, largely because they are regarded as racial, as opposed to ethnic, groups (Bhui 1999). On one extreme, important factors relating to culture, ethnicity and faith are often simply overlooked; on the opposite extreme, ethnicity, culture and faith are assumed to provide a single, all-explanatory framework in the aetiology of social and mental health problems for people belonging to ethnic minority groups (Bhugra and Bhui 1999).

Discourses about culture, ethnicity and race are the subject of extensive debate in the social sciences. In recent times, these debates have extended to encompass faith and its relation to ethnicity and identity. In particular, the significance of ethnicity and faith in relation to identity amongst British Muslims is complex. In recent times the 'identity', loyalty and affiliations of young British Muslims have come under relentless scrutiny, whereby as a group they have been inadvertently homogenised and pathologised for the very real challenges and problems they deal with. As young individuals, many young British Muslims report a sense that mainstream civic and community engagement with them only occurs in the context of their being viewed as a problem, demanding unprecedented remedial measures and interventions, or as a 'high risk' group that requires constant management – not as respected individual stakeholders who have much to contribute and offer to wider society. For individuals and communities to participate and make a contribution to wider public life, they must be able to identify key public institutions as their own. Nowhere is this more important than the provision of services which are usually the first point of contact between citizens and the state.

Consistently over the last 5 years, the Muslim Youth Helpline (MYH) has reported that 'Relationships' comprise the most pressing concern dealt with on the helpline – hence the focus of this report. Young Muslims often find themselves caught between a traditional community which views most youth issues as taboo, and a mainstream secular society that fails to provide appropriate support, both factors thus impacting negatively on their identity. A fractured identity, together with a lack of a sense of belonging, will affect a young person's self esteem and emotional wellbeing, inhibiting civic participation. As is reflected in this report, young British Muslims who contact MYH describe intergenerational conflict (and teenage relationships) as a central issue, indicating that they are experiencing difficulties negotiating their space and making sense of the world around them.

Yet the solution for these young people is clearly neither to reject their tradition or culture associated with their family, nor to reject wider British society, but rather to develop a space in which the two can meet harmoniously and constructively. This can only be achieved by exploring the complex root causes of the issues that young British Muslims deal with, resulting from the interplay and interconnectedness of a myriad of factors such as faith, identity, culture, gender and wider social inequalities.

Akeela Ahmed
Chief Executive, Muslim Youth Helpline (MYH)

Executive Summary

Problems

It is very common for young people to describe problems or concerns relating to relationships. On the Muslim Youth Helpline (MYH), this topic is the biggest single area of concern for callers, encompassing diverse aspects including:

- **Boy-girl relationships**
  Relationship problems between young people, before or outside of marriage, are commonly reported: these may be exacerbated if a young person feels that they cannot discuss such relationships with their family and friends (especially if such relationships cross faith, cultural or ethnic boundaries.)

- **Marriage**
  This category encompasses a diverse set of problems. Some young people wish to get married and are finding the process difficult; others want to stay single but are being pressured into marriage. This pressure is linked both to family and to wider society, especially for women. A consistent but limited proportion also describe being forced into marriage. Some of those who are married report marital problems, including domestic abuse.

- **Family**
  Concerns relating to the family account for 10–15 percent of all relationship enquiries. A wide range of pressures are reported, from marriage to work and academic achievement. Prominent in our research were problems in the relationships between mothers-in-law and daughters-in-law, especially where the daughter-in-law has come from abroad and lacks a support network in Britain.

- **Community**
  The wider Muslim community, including friends and extended families, can be a crucial factor in decision-making for young people, at times as a constraining influence. Some young people report being afraid to take certain decisions, such as divorcing their spouse, out of concern about the possible negative reaction of the community which could affect their family.

- **Sexual Abuse**
  This is a small but consistent concern on the helpline. Most often, callers who report sexual abuse are adults who have been psychologically affected by abuse that took place when they were children. The helpline has also received calls where child sexual abuse is ongoing.

- **Sexuality**
  Concerns over sexuality are fairly common, especially from young male callers. Such concerns can present acute problems for young people who feel pressure from their families and communities to enter into a traditional marriage.

Recommendations

- **Faith and cultural sensitivity**
  A sensitivity to faith and culture is crucial in helping young people from Muslim communities with relationship problems. There is an urgent need to go beyond a merely abstract conception of the issues – service providers should try to understand how faith, culture and society interact in creating the framework within which choices are made for individual people. Such interaction can often vary substantially for different people, and even for the same person at different stages in their life.

- **Knowledge and understanding**
  Providers should make themselves aware of the basic tenets of the Muslim faith, as well as the ceremonies and traditions of the communities (such as the Indian, Pakistani and Bangladeshi communities) with whom they are working.

- **Avoiding stereotypes**
  Service providers, especially helpline workers, emphasised the negative role that stereotyping can play in service provision. In particular, participants criticised the stereotypes which pathologise the Muslim family, such as an exaggerated notion that young Muslim women lack freedom and have all choices made for them by male members of their family.

Statutory service providers

- **Language provision**
  All the statutory providers we spoke to emphasised the importance of providing adequate language services for recent immigrants who do not speak English, as a language barrier can make the provision of services much more difficult.

- **Understanding the needs of women**
  Access to female doctors was identified as an important need for some women who will not otherwise access services. Providers also suggested that more can be done for them to encourage women, especially those who are recent immigrants, to engage in social interaction and healthier lifestyles – such as by providing spaces for physical exercise and healthy cooking classes – which could significantly improve their health and the health of their families.

- **Sensitivity training**
  Training around faith and cultural sensitivity could be extended for some statutory providers. It was suggested that voluntary post-qualification training could be set up for doctors who wish to learn more about the communities with whom they are working, which could help them to provide a more holistic level of care. Examples of providers who have voluntarily undertaken to learn about diverse communities could be highlighted as examples of best practice.

Specialist services

The need for specialist services with a dedicated focus on Muslim communities in the UK was reiterated frequently in the research as one of the key ways to deal with the relationship problems of young Muslims:

- **Listening**
  GPs tended to be very strongly in favour of services such as MYH, which provide a level of pastoral and emotional support that many primary care providers simply do not have the resources or level of specialisation to provide.

- **Counselling**
  Many young people facing relationship difficulties will not access primary care or psychological services until their problems are at a very advanced stage. As a result, it is important for young Muslims to be able to speak to a counsellor about problems relating to family, marriage, or relationships. There is a need for both specialist Muslim counsellors, and mainstream counsellors who are trained in faith and cultural sensitivity.

- **Mediation**
  The need to expand and increase the use of Muslim mediation services was frequently suggested during the research. Many participants said that social services can, in some cases, be too quick to suggest more advanced courses of action. It was generally agreed that mediation should at least be considered as a possibility when dealing with problems in marriage, or between parents and children, in Muslim communities.

The key problems identified with existing mediation services were:

Lack of funding and access
Lack of investment has clearly limited access to mediation services: funding has not been as forthcoming as it could be from statutory bodies, charitable trusts, or the Muslim community itself. Government agencies in particular were seen as being more likely to fund projects that look impressive but are in fact of a short-term and low-impact nature.

Need for greater understanding
It was suggested that mainstream mediation services could use an adaptive approach when working with Muslim families, taking into account what can often be strong family bonds and an unwillingness to split apart. Some also suggested that awareness of mediation, including informal mediation via family or friends, could be improved.

Under-representation of young people
Existing mediation services were sometimes perceived as being too focused on older members of the community, with the result being that young people are under-represented. Without youth representation in mediation, young people will feel the services are skewed against them. Mediation services need to dispel this idea by taking positive action to understand young people's perspectives.

Introduction

For ten years, the Muslim Youth Helpline (MYH) has been in operation as a support service for young British Muslims, taking daily calls on a diverse range of issues. The biggest single concern for callers has consistently been 'relationships': boyfriends/girlfriends, marriage, parents, family or community. Yet very little research has been conducted on this topic.

This report aims to give service providers, particularly those who work with young people from Muslim communities, useful information on the kind of issues that confront young people. A brief literature review outlines existing relevant work, and quantitative data from the MYH Electronic Logging System (ELS) is provided and analysed. To gain a more in-depth understanding, we have also conducted a number of focus groups and interviews, speaking to young people from London but also to GPs, volunteer helpline workers and a voluntary service provider. This information is brought together in the two main sections of the report: 'Problems' and 'Dealing with Problems'.

The first section, 'Problems', outlines the issues which have been reported by service users and divides them according to their proportional weighting over the period 2006–2010. This section provides the necessary background for those who wish to understand the main types of issues that have been reported, as well as which problems are more prevalent and which are less common. Interviews in this section give details of particular cases and the perspectives of individual interviewees, while case studies present an in-depth look at a helpline case in each of the major categories. The second section, 'Dealing with Problems', suggests the ways in which service provision for young people can be improved. This takes into account the issues described in the previous section, and the suggestions that have been proposed by existing service providers. They are organised according to the type of provider for whom they apply (general, statutory and specialist), the aim being to provide useful suggestions for all providers.

The helpline is our key source of information, providing quantitative data over a period of four years, as well as case studies and interviews with helpline volunteers. This information is used to outline the main relationships issues faced by young people, as well as their relative prevalence and change over time. As the only helpline of its type in the UK, and with a steadily increasing number of clients (see Fig. 3, p.21), the information gained here should be particularly useful to those interested in understanding the diverse concerns of young British people from Muslim communities. The information is also strengthened by service provider interviews, which have provided details on those particular issues with which these providers have relevant experience.

Although the helpline itself is a national service, and receives calls from across the country, this report has a broad focus on London (though with clear national implications), as a central aim of the report is to provide information and a basis for training for those service providers based in London. It would be useful to replicate elements of the research in this report in other parts of the country, particularly in major cities like Manchester, Bradford and Birmingham. This would enable a comparison between areas of the UK, looking at the relative prevalence of issues.

Literature review

While the amount of research on Muslim communities in the UK has increased recently, forming quite a large body of literature, work specifically focused on young Muslims remains more limited. We present here a selective review, emphasising work that is relevant to the topic of this report.

The previous piece of research produced by MYH was conducted in conjunction with the National Youth Agency in 2007, *Providing Faith and Culturally Sensitive Support Services to Young British Muslims.* It was authored by Rabia Malik, Aaliyah Shaikh, and Mustafa Suleyman. Their report employed a mixture of quantitative and qualitative data analysis, including interviews with service users and volunteer helpline workers, to give recommendations to those providing services to young British Muslims. They found the position of young British Muslims to be that of a heterogeneous and diverse group facing similar challenges to all other young people, but additionally facing greater social disadvantages, discrimination, and alienation, all of which have the potential to increase psychological vulnerability. It was found to be important for many Muslim service users that the infusion of Islam within their lives was recognised in the support they were offered. The report emphasised the importance of service provision that is not faith-based, but is faith-sensitive: '[F]or both clients and volunteers, Islam held different meanings as a personal, social and ethical identity. To omit it, however, from conversations and support work is to deny a significant part of young Muslims' experiences' (Malik et al. 2007: 46). More investment was recommended in data and research, as well as the increased use of faith as a key indicator by mainstream service providers. The report also includes a full outline of MYH and the services it provides, and we have thus tried to avoid reproducing similar material here (see also Fulat and Jaffrey 2006).

Muslim communities: society and relationships

A detailed series of reports commissioned by the Department for Communities and Local Government and published by the Change Institute (2008), *Understanding Muslim Ethnic Communities*, provides useful and recent demographic data on British Muslim communities. Some of the key findings of the Summary Report (pp. 6-24) are particularly relevant to this study, including the fact that approximately 50 percent of England's Muslim community lives in London, where Muslim communities make up over 8 percent of the population.

As a group, these communities were found to be more likely to face socioeconomic disadvantage, and some were found to experience 'multiple discrimination based on place of origin, racial and national stereotypes.' Muslim communities in areas of high deprivation were found to face high levels of disadvantage and unmet needs with regard to a wide range of issues, including: educational underachievement, poor health, high unemployment, hate crime, poor housing conditions, and segregation in housing and education. All these factors can exacerbate relationship problems, as structural socioeconomic inequality and disadvantage can bring about psychological as well as material consequences (see Lynch et al. 2000).

A report commissioned by the Greater London Authority (2006) builds on this demographic detail in the context of Greater London. The report also discusses socioeconomic profiles, Muslims in public life, the criminal justice system and Islamophobia. The 2001 Census found that 50 percent of the Muslim population in London was under the age of 24, younger than the average age of the population of London as a whole. Muslims aged 16-24 have, as a group, lower qualification levels and higher unemployment rates in comparison to the general population. A similar pattern is replicated elsewhere in Britain, particularly in areas with higher proportions of immigrant communities (see Abbas 2005).

This demographic detail forms the social context of the communities being studied in this report. It demonstrates the importance of avoiding the essentialisation of concerns by treating them as 'products' of religion or culture: the issues explored here take place in a complex context incorporating a multitude of factors, socioeconomic as well as cultural and religious.

Young Muslim perspectives

Community projects have produced useful reports which outline the issues identified by young Muslims as significant: the Young Muslim Voices (YMV) *Project Report* (2008/9), for example, identified a number of 'critical issues' raised by young Muslims in Islington. Many of these were externally imposed, including high levels of anti-Muslim racism, stereotyping, marginalisation and profiling via anti-terror laws. Concerns raised by the young people that relate to the topic of this report included: parental involvement, cultural factors, education, employment, as well as concerns specific to girls and young women who identified family pressures over marriage as a key concern.

A recent report by Sughra Ahmed from the Policy Research Centre (2009), *Seen and Not Heard: Voices of Young British Muslims*, is particularly useful in identifying and expanding upon areas of concern for young Muslims. As well as similar issues emerging to those described in the YMV report, Ahmed also found that young people demonstrated a wide range of approaches to relationships: young people interviewed in Scotland, for example, expressed their support for arranged marriages, while female research participants in Tower Hamlets said that they did not tell their families about male friends as a result of their parents' strict attitudes towards mixed-gender activity, and some said they struggled against the wishes of their parents with regard to arranged marriages.

Marriage, family and community

Almost all the research on marriage and family relationships for young Muslims is centred on the experiences of South Asian communities, with the unfortunate result that other Muslim communities are underrepresented. (Typically, the term 'South Asian' refers to communities originating from Bangladesh, India, Nepal, Pakistan and Sri Lanka; sometimes Afghanistan is also included, as well as some smaller neighbouring countries.) Most of the existing work on marriage also emerges from an emphasis on women which, though perhaps justified, does not always accord with research (including our own) showing that young men can often be just as likely to face problems over marriage.

Cultural perceptions of marriage differ: many South Asian and some African cultures traditionally give parents a significant role in affecting their children's decisions relating to marriage, including timing and choice of partner. Young people from these communities have different experiences and views on the topic. Some vigorously defend marriage customs and say their views correspond to those of their parents, while others say they feel constrained or coerced by what they see as a gap in attitudes between the generations.

In a detailed study, Gangoli et al. (2006) found that while arranged marriages were viewed by interviewees as an important part of South Asian culture, often perceived to have various advantages over other types of relationships, forced marriages – defined as those where the consent of one or both of the partners has not been obtained – were seen as unacceptable and based on the misinterpretation of cultural and religious practices. Pressures over marriage were found to exist for both men and women. Although both men and women assumed marriage to entail significant parental input, young men were seen as having more freedom than women over their choice of marriage partner. Overall, however, most research participants felt that there was flexibility and choice for them in marriage, though within parameters. Charsley and Shaw (2006) found that some women from Pakistani communities reported negative experiences of transnational marriage, particularly issues around desertion.

On the issue of forced marriage in particular, a report was produced by the Home Office Working Group on Forced Marriage (2000). Participants agreed that forced marriage is not a religious issue but a cultural one, often emphasising that while the practice exists across different religious groups and ethnic communities, it is not acceptable in any major world religion. A clear distinction was drawn by participants between forced and arranged marriage. Key motivations for forced marriages were found to be: peer group or family pressure, attempting to strengthen family links, protecting perceived cultural and religious ideals, preventing 'unsuitable' relationships (such as those outside a particular ethnic, cultural, religious or caste group), perceptions of family honour, long-standing family commitments, and controlling female behaviour and sexuality.

The experiences of young British Muslims in relation to the cultural and religious practices of their communities vary. Some are keen to maintain existing tradition, even to strengthen it, while others find it restrictive. Many find themselves negotiating a space somewhere in the middle. 'Muslim' identities are constructed in complex, sometimes conflicting, ways, including as a positive assertion and in response to racism, amongst many other factors (Archer 2001; Basit 1997; see also Malik 2006). In a study of British Muslim women and attitudes to education, Ahmad (2001) found that young women were constantly renegotiating their cultural, religious, and personal identities, and that such processes operated in complex, and sometimes contradictory, ways. Attitudes to relationships form one of the major areas of negotiation: South Asian communities, for example, are likely to frown upon premarital relationships and emphasise the importance of the parental role in selecting marriage partners; the general British attitude varies, but tends to involve the family less in the choice of a partner, and also places less emphasis on the necessity of marriage for a relationship to be accepted.

Young people going against the wishes of their parents can also face more indirect forms of pressure. Research focusing specifically on this subject, however, is still very limited, and much of the current evidence is either confined to South Asian communities outside the UK (see Samuel 2010, which used interviews to assess inter-generational attitudes to relationships within South Asian communities in Canada, finding that dating outside the community is fairly common but often kept secret from the family), or remains anecdotal.

Stereotypes

While participants in the research often acknowledge they may have different views from their parents, they tend to forcefully challenge stereotypes about the way marriages take place in their communities. There is some substantial work on the popular and dominant perception of arranged marriages as having a worrying tendency toward pathologising the Asian family, and in particular representing young Asian women as weak and powerless victims (Dwyer 2000, see also Brah & Minhas 1985, Puar 1994).

Not only is this representation of Asian women generally incorrect, it is also disempowering. Research with young Muslims, especially girls and young women, often brings out the frustration of those who feel they are not permitted to define themselves, but must submit to a dominant (and unflattering) view of them imposed from outside. As Burr (2002: 836) notes, the power of stereotypes of South Asian cultures goes beyond cultural prejudices; particularly with regard to mental illness, such dominant stereotypes can 'become incorporated as pseudo scientific explanations that are then incorporated as fact and used to account for different patterns of health and illness' (see also Burr & Chapman 2004). See Coppock and Hopton (2000) for an outline of the connctedness of racism and mental health. Some studies have found, for example, that teachers can have strongly negative stereotypes of Muslim children, assuming their families to be authoritarian and repressive, and that this can affect the way in which Muslim children are treated at school (Ballard 1994; Verma et al. 1994; cited in Archer 2001). Stereotypes of Muslim women in particular have been found to 'impact on their daily lives' and affect the quality of the services they receive, particularly those relating to higher education and careers advice (Tyrer and Ahmed 2006).

Services

Services which can help young people with relationship problems include primary care services, psychological services, mediation, counselling and gender-specific services. All of these services, except primary care, can be run by public, private and voluntary providers. For those from Muslim communities – particularly women – such services, if they exist, can be more difficult to access than for the general population.

There is a large body of literature examining the many factors which can make access to services more difficult, and it is beyond the scope of this review to outline them all. Specifically regarding Muslim communities, key concerns that have been highlighted include the lack of language support and female support staff, as well as the importance of cultural and faith sensitivity. For example, *The Afghan Muslim Community in England* (2009) report details the problems Afghan women in Britain can face in asserting independence, and a particular concern was found to be the lack of English language teaching provision. Combined with cultural pressures, this can increase a sense of isolation for women and exacerbate serious relationship problems which already exist. The lack of English language provision can be a serious problem especially in light of the fact that many people from Muslim communities in Britain are first-generation immigrants. As a result, these groups can often find it most difficult to access services (see also: Roberts 2006; Mogra 2006).

Support for South Asian women experiencing domestic violence or forced marriage in the North-East was found to be limited in the context of a general lack of services for BME women, especially first-generation immigrant women. There is, therefore, a strong need for more culturally sensitive services in this area (Gangoli et al. 2006). The Home Office Working Group on Forced Marriage has suggested that personal safety, confidentiality and accurate information about rights and choices are basic needs that should always be considered, while 'challenging and changing people's attitudes' provides the key to preventing forced marriages (Home Office 2000: 20). Further guidelines are recommended for service providers and local government authorities.

The literature on service provision for BME communities generally supports the idea that while the accessibility of such services varies according to region, it is found to be lacking overall and needs to be improved. Recent work by Bhui (2010) suggests that assessment, particularly for mental health services, should include a cultural assessment that takes into account aspects of religious identity, and should be conducted by culturally and religiously-informed practitioners. Such methods are not yet widespread.

Methodology

Quantitative analysis

MYH possesses a unique source of quantitative data, the Electronic Logging System (ELS), which provides a strictly confidential record of information for every call received. This includes the date and time of the call, the name of the helpline worker taking the call, the caller's details (age, gender, ethnicity, and location), and the category and sub-category of the call. There is also space for detailed notes to be made by the helpline worker on the nature of each call and the suggestions made by the helpline worker.

This record provides a highly useful source of information on the concerns of the young people who call the helpline. Demographic information is less consistently recorded, as callers are free to refuse to provide such details.

Calls are logged into one of fourteen categories, ranging from Education & Employment to Mental Health and Religion (see Fig.1, p.20). The Relationships category, on which this report focuses, is itself divided into the following twelve sub-categories (see Fig.2, p.21):

- Marriage and divorce
- Boy/girl concerns
- Family pressures
- Parents
- Friends
- Forced marriage
- Pre-marital concerns
- Children
- Bereavement
- Other
- Domestic violence
- Siblings

Call logs were analysed for this report over a five-year period (from 2005–2010) and provided information regarding both the relative significance to the callers of particular categories, and the changes that have taken place over a number of years.

Qualitative analysis

There were four different sources for qualitative data: interviews with helpline workers, interviews with service providers, helpline case studies, and a focus group with young people.

Interviews with helpline workers

Quantitative analysis, though useful, does not illustrate in depth the types of problems that can occur across categories of calls. Here, experienced helpline volunteers were an insightful source of information about the concerns of callers, especially as all of those who were interviewed have been volunteering on the helpline for a number of years. (Names have been changed to protect confidentiality.)

Interviews were semi-structured and open-ended, lasting 30–45 minutes with scope for interviewee-led responses and digressions. Questions were based on the ELS categorisation and academic literature. Interviews were recorded and transcribed, then categorised and analysed with the other qualitative data to identify the themes on which the latter two sections of this report are based.

Service provider interviews

Broadening the scope of Malik et al (2007), London-based service providers were also interviewed for this report in order to understand concerns which might be different to those experienced on the helpline. This was particularly important in discussing how service provision might be improved.

Interviews were semi-structured and open-ended and lasted 1–2 hours on average; as with the helpline worker interviews, they were based on a set of questions formulated on the basis of previous work. A large-scale survey was not possible due to time and cost limitations, so key providers were selected as follows:

a) Two general practitioners, based in Hackney and Tower Hamlets respectively, provided the perspective of statutory primary care providers working in London boroughs with large Muslim populations.

b) One voluntary service provider, a co-founder of the Muslim Mediation Service (MMS), provided the perspective of a voluntary provider working with Muslim communities in London.

Helpline case studies

Helpline records were also used to provide qualitative analysis, building on the quantitative work and the interviews to provide examples of cases being discussed. Individual cases were discussed with helpline workers familiar with them. Some details have been changed to protect confidentiality.

Focus group with young people

A group of young people was recruited, mostly from London, to provide a perspective of young people from Muslim communities. Open-ended questions were asked and personal experiences were discussed in depth. The young people were aged between 14 and 21, and represented a variety of different communities including Pakistani, Indian, Somali, Egyptian and African-Indian. The London boroughs represented were Ealing, Hammersmith and Fulham, North Greenwich, Barnet, Newham, and Westminster; those outside London were Buckinghamshire and Luton.

Problems

The concerns of helpline service users at MYH are recorded onto a detailed, confidential logging system (ELS) which can be used to analyse data over a period of years. Figure 1 shows a breakdown of all helpline calls by category during the period 2006–2010 with relationships constituting the largest single concern of callers during this period (at 29 percent of all calls). These callers were most often aged between 23 and 25 years, but a significant number of them were younger than twenty (see Fig.4, p.22). The number of individual service users rose during the same period, from less than 350 to over 400 per year, following the successful implementation of a post-2006 policy to limit the number of calls per person. Helpline workers often stated that relationship concerns, though individually categorised on the helpline, tend to be intertwined with other issues.

> When it comes to relationships, it's more or less the case that it's a by-product of a lot of other problems, and with Muslim clients it tends to be surrounded by family pressures, the cultural influences of how new relationships should be formed, whether it be marriage or friendships. (Rahim, 22, helpline worker)

Fig. 1 - Helpline calls by category, 2006 – 2010

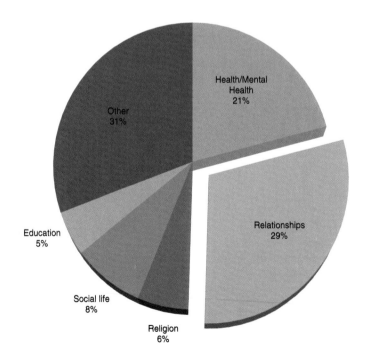

Fig. 2 - Relationship enquiries by category, 2006 – 2010

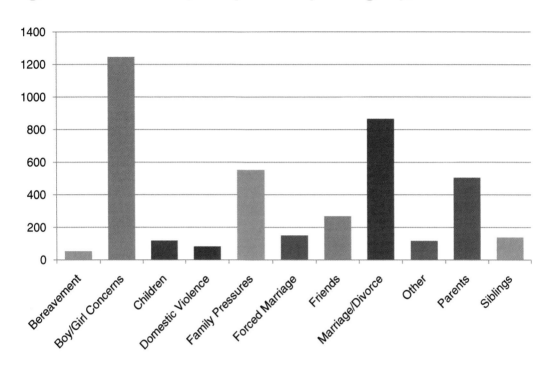

Fig. 3 - Number of helpline service users, 2006 – 2010

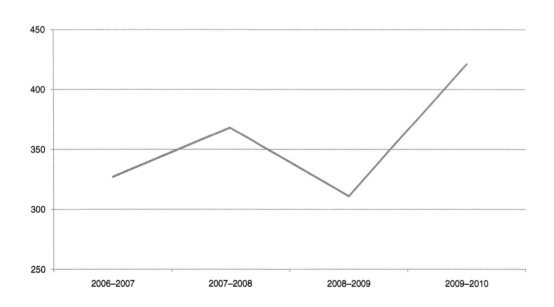

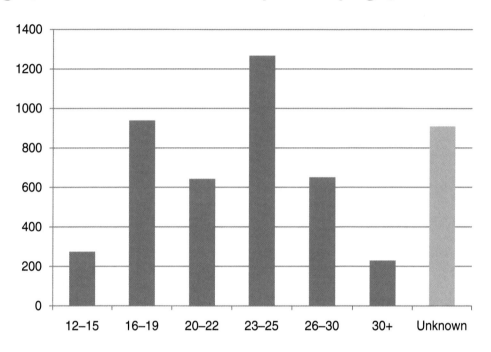

Fig. 4 - Number of relationship calls by age, 2006 – 2010

Both the quantitative data and the helpline workers interviewed suggested specific areas of prominence within the relationships category, including: parents, friends, marriage, divorce, sexual abuse and sexuality. Figure 2 examines the breakdown of relationship enquiries, showing the number of enquiries per category over the past four years. (This is not the same as the number of individual callers, as one caller may make multiple enquiries relating to a variety of issues). Boy-girl concerns were clearly the biggest concern over this period, followed by Marriage, Family Pressures, and Parents, respectively. In this section, the quantitative data is built upon by taking these key concerns as the major headings, with Parents being incorporated into the Family section, and with the addition of a further category, Community, which arose from the qualitative interviews.

Boy-girl relationships

Boy-girl concerns – calls regarding a heterosexual relationship outside of marriage – are very common on the helpline, and constitute between one-fifth and one-third of all relationship calls, depending on the year (see Fig.5, p.24). This suggests such relationships are not unusual and can be a significant cause for concern for young people from Muslim communities. The content of these calls varies across a range of issues including questions over the legitimacy of such relationships, the family and community pressure surrounding them (see Family and Community below), the problems and disagreements within a relationship itself, concern over the future of a relationship, and so on.

Some young people contact MYH because they feel unable to discuss such relationships with their

Case study

Hawra is a British teenager from an Arab background who suffered various forms of abuse, including violent abuse, at the hands of her former boyfriend. She first contacted MYH after reporting him to the police and she is currently pursuing charges against him. He has continued to call and threaten her with violence if she does not drop the charges.

She has not received any support from her family, despite informing them of the abuse, as they feel her having previously been in a relationship has brought shame onto the family. As a result of this pressure, Hawra has even considered dropping the charges and marrying her ex-boyfriend.

MYH have supported her by providing a safe space to discuss her concerns. Additionally, she has found the support provided by MYH has enabled her to develop a sense of connection with the community. MYH have also supported her efforts to obtain the legal assistance she needs through other agencies and bodies.

parents or siblings. In these cases, rather than the relationship itself constituting a problem, it is the need to talk to someone – and the difficulty in talking to the usual people – that pushes someone to consult a helpline service. Helpline workers thought that the use of friends as a support network varied depending on the individual person. Some young people were very open with their friends about relationships with the opposite sex, while others found it more difficult to speak to their friends, particularly if they thought their friends might disapprove.

> That's why they usually call us because we're around the same age or a little bit older so they feel they can, after realising everything is confidential, we're like an outlet for them ... Most of it is between girlfriend/boyfriend issues, they don't feel comfortable talking to their parents about it. They don't feel comfortable talking to their older siblings about it either. (Sana, 24, helpline worker)

Being unable to discuss an informal relationship often means having to keep secrets, and this can sometimes create a pressing need to formalise such a relationship through marriage. A helpline worker described receiving a number of calls, from girls or young women in particular, involved in the early stages of a relationship and eager to get married. Such callers, who are often below the age of twenty, have difficulty convincing their parents to approve of early marriage, and discuss eloping with their partner as an alternative option.

> They want to get married really young and they've found someone but their parents aren't happy with that particular person. But they're really young and they've literally only known

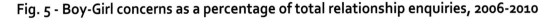

Fig. 5 - Boy-Girl concerns as a percentage of total relationship enquiries, 2006-2010

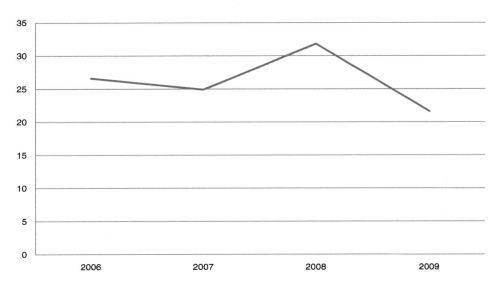

them for a couple of months or something ... I've only had one or two where it's really seri-ous and they're going to run away. Majority of them, it's quite lighthearted, they would have a bust up with their family [and] that's why they would call, just to vent really because they have no person to vent out on. So they would kind of be quite continuous, they would carry on seeing whoever, and then their parents would find out they'd come back, then they'd go, it's more like a cycle. **(Malika, 19, helpline worker)**

This concern over unapproved relationships was reiterated by the young people we spoke to. The group agreed that such relationships could often cause problems, describing cases where boys and girls who are keen to get married have had difficulty convincing their parents to approve such a course of action. Such relationships may cross cultural and faith boundaries, said one participant, which could constitute another topic of concern.

What I've come across is you get some people who are in relationships where they genuinely like each other and they want to develop it into something more serious, some people straight away want to get married, but they don't because they're considered as too young to even consider marriage. So they have this relationship and hide it from everyone ... Another thing to bear in mind is that relationships Muslims have are not always with Muslims. Sometimes they are with non-Muslims. So that's definitely another problem, especially if they want to develop it into something more serious like marriage. That's definitely an issue because they don't know how they'd go about doing that. They do have that problem, not so much the boys who want to marry a non-Muslim, more the girls. **(Alina, 21, helpline worker)**

Concerns about relationships are a common part of growing up for all young people, but those from Muslim communities can face additional difficulties due to stricter cultural attitudes towards relation-ships before marriage. Some may feel they have to keep their relationships a secret from their family and even friends, fearing disapproval, and common concerns about relationships can thus be exacerbated through lack of access to the usual sources of support. Where young people are prevented from engaging in either a pre-marital relationship or marriage, they can often feel frustrated, stressed and worried.

Marriage

As well as relationships before marriage constituting a major topic, the helpline receives a substantial number of calls relating to marriage itself, a topic which overtook boy-girl concerns in 2009–2010 to become the number one relationship issue for callers. This has remained a fairly steady concern on the helpline (at between 15–25 percent) through the years 2006–2009. Forced marriage has, seperately, been a consistent concern at around 4 percent of all enquiries per year. Taken together with boy-girl concerns (see above), these two issues alone sometimes represent 50 percent of all the relationship calls taken in a year. But this does not mean the concerns of callers are uniform: pressures surrounding marriage affect different people in a variety of ways.

Many young people call the helpline because they want to get married, but are unable to do so for various reasons. In many Muslim communities, marriage is seen as a necessary prerequisite to a legitimate relationship. This may explain why marriage is a major topic of concern for young people who call the helpline. Helpline workers said that a significant subset of callers on this topic were young men with mental health problems, who had encountered difficulties in finding a partner due to the stigma associated with mental illness.

> With a lot of our clients, we've got a lot of mid-20s, male, mental health issues, wanting to get married but can't – because of all of the above. (Sana, 24, helpline worker)

> There's a lot of concerns regarding marriage, a lot of people looking for marriage, almost desperate for it. We have a lot of calls from men and women in different stages of their lives, looking for marriage and struggling to find it for a massive variety of reasons. A lot of the time you'll find it's linked to mental health, I've found more with men who have mental health issues and are seeking marriage, which they're finding very difficult. (Rahim, 22, helpline worker)

Young men in this situation are likely to be accessing general mental health services, but they may feel that these services are too broad in their remit to be able to address their specific marriage concerns. Where the young person discusses these concerns, they may, nevertheless, feel that the problem was not fully addressed, particularly if they think the service provider does not understand the cultural implications of remaining unmarried in their community.

Marriage concerns are, of course, not limited to young men. Female callers were described as being less likely to have mental health problems, but still likely to call with problems surrounding marriage, sometimes with issues similar to those of the young male callers and relating to difficulties in finding a partner. This is especially the case for female callers in their late twenties or early thirties. However,

Case study

Hisham is a 27-year-old British man who has been married for the past six months. Hisham's marriage was arranged by his parents, but he had previously spoken to the girl before agreeing to marry her. After the marriage, Hicham found his wife to be distant and unwilling to spend time with him. It later transpired that she had previously been in a relationship with another man, whom she had wanted to marry, but whom her parents had rejected.

Hisham's wife said that despite the marriage, she still wanted to be with the man with whom she was previously in a relationship. Hisham found this very difficult and raised the matter with his family. He is now separated from his wife and they are considering their options.

Hisham contacted MYH as he found it difficult to talk to any of his friends and family about the emotions he was experiencing. Talking to MYH allowed Hisham to be honest and to express his feelings without a sense of being judged or ashamed. Hisham was able to explore the impact of his relationship with his wife on himself as well as explore the options available to him.

helpline workers said that female callers often do not encounter problems in finding a partner *per se*, but in the specificity of the partner they are being encouraged to look for:

> If they're in their late twenties, there's a trend where they either don't know how to get married, or the difficulty of living in this country but having the pressures of a specific type of person they have to marry, depending on their background. **(Farooq, 24, helpline worker)**

Helpline workers also explained that callers often feel pressure to get married, but that only a small minority of these situations could be properly termed as 'forced marriage'. In communities where arranged marriages are common, young people may be undecided about whether they want to make use of traditional community networks for finding a partner or not, especially if they are additionally unsure whether they are ready for marriage.

> I think people misunderstand what you mean by forced marriage. Sometimes people say, my parents are trying to get me married, but not actually forced marriage, they're just saying: you've graduated, maybe it's time for you to think about marriage – but that's the natural progression of life: you go to school, you get married, you have kids. Maybe we don't all want to follow that, but a lot of people do tend to follow it, so in that sense they feel pressured. **(Sana, 24, helpline worker)**

> Sometimes the girl, they're saying, you've seen so many guys, you need to pick one. Or we get calls from guys even, saying I've seen loads of girls, but I just don't find them attractive,

Fig. 6 - Marriage concerns as a percentage of total relationship enquiries, 2006-2010

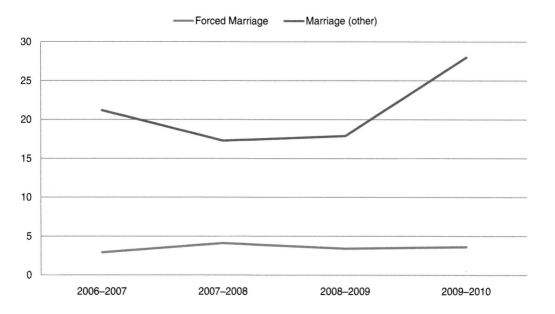

or they don't want to get married, but they're feeling pressured by it. (**Aaliyah, 25, helpline worker**)

A lot of them are just not sure whether they should go [abroad for marriage] or not or – whether they should take that step with someone who they don't know very well, whether they should trust their parents … Usually, they trust their parents and they're not getting forced or anything like that, they're quite happy and content. (**Alina, 21, helpline worker**)

This pressure can, in some cases, amount to a forced marriage, which is categorised separately on the helpline and has appeared as a consistent issue, at just under 5 percent per year. In the classic forced marriage scenario, a young person is worried that he or she will be forced into a marriage in the future. The helpline does receive calls of this nature. A much less discussed phenomenon, however, is the prevalence of complications for those who have been through such marriages and subsequently left their partners. People in this situation can be left with a host of psychological and mental health issues: they may have only gradually come to an understanding that they were forced into the marriage, and they have commonly lost trust in their families, contributing to a sense of isolation which is made worse if their families have reacted negatively to their decision to end the marriage.

We do get a lot of people who do get forced – whether they are about to get forced or they have already been forced. They've come back, it's been a couple of years and they're not with their partner anymore and they have had no one to talk to about that particular experience. That what we usually talk about, and that's the start of a really long process. (**Sana, 24, helpline worker**)

Both the service providers we interviewed and the young people we spoke to said that while service provision was available to prevent an imminent forced marriage from taking place, they did not think it was available for those who are dealing with the psychological after-effects of forced marriage, or for those whose concerns over forced marriage do not fit the classic scenario. One young person described in the focus group the difficulties she faced in trying to prevent the forced marriage of a friend:

> I've actually had a friend in that position, and as a friend you find you can't do much ... What we tried to do was try to get her point across to the parents, a lot of time to her siblings, because we thought they would be more understanding ... You have to give them all the practical information, so helpline numbers ... When you're running out of options and there's nothing else to do, if they want to leave, it's their decision, so provide them with information. The problem a lot of the time is their mindset, so for example my friend went through this, she could not stand against her parents. Not because she was quiet, she wasn't – she was loud – but because all her life she was being groomed into doing what they said. (Asma, 21)

In addition to the forced marriage concerns, some young callers experience problems managing their expectations of marriage, particularly those who are newly married:

> When most people get married, they see it as the natural progression – it's that next part of turning into an adult. But when you're confined into a certain space, confined into doing certain roles and activities, it puts pressure on you and the marriage, and we do get calls about how they're finding it difficult to cope with all these pressures. It's difficult for a lot of the clients to see a way out, they don't see a way out ... They kind of just get on with it. (Malika, 19, helpline worker)

Marriage is also a factor in some domestic abuse cases, where the strength of pressure from the wider family was suggested in some cases to be acting to prevent women from leaving situations of domestic abuse. This was especially the case where women are living with in-laws (see 'Family', below), as described by a GP during an interview.

> Husband beating wife, husband neglecting wife or emotionally abusing wife ... And relationship problems as in, women who are just really vulnerable and dominated by their husband, and don't really have a voice. That's quite common. But they're very trapped, because often they have children. They'll never leave, even if they're being abused, because they haven't got any other family here, so you can't really do the same sort of things as you do with non-Asians, because [non-Asians are] often happy to leave their families and go into a refuge. Whereas these ladies aren't. They fear that they'll never get married again, or their children will get taken away. (Rukaiya, 33, GP in Tower Hamlets)

> There's not much you can do about it because these women are quite isolated when they're here. They don't have much a voice. They would never admit it to the doctor, I think it would be quite shameful for them. So we're often just left seeing them time and time again, saying what's the problem today? ... So you just talk to them and show them a bit of kindness. (Masood, 27, GP in Hackney)

Family

Approximately 10–15 percent of all relationship enquiries over the past four years have included, as their main concern, family relationships, making this (proportionally) the third biggest issue in the relationship category. As noted above, family relationships can also be a factor in marriage and relationship problems. Families, of course, have a large and complex presence in the lives of many young people. Helpline workers often stressed the significant role that families can play in solving problems, as well as the importance of the family for improving the situation (notably the mental health) of a young person. Though the helpline does receive calls relating to severe familial problems, such as domestic violence and abuse, callers also report a variety of other concerns – at times, for example, searching for better ways to communicate with their parents, or describing family pressures which are exacerbating other problems, especially to do with marriage.

> You've also got family pressures, which is a very big thing – which can be in all aspects of your life, in your relationship with your siblings, with your parents. With regards to marriage it can be because of your studies, or your mental health issues which they don't understand.
> (Aaliyah, 25, helpline worker)

Family pressures can be especially difficult to deal with for young people when they relate to school, university, and marriage. BME parents have been found in other studies to emphasise academic achievement comparatively more than other parents, with the result that BME children and young people are more likely to feel 'very pushed' by their parents (DCSF 2003: 5). This can create pressure on a young person which they may feel is undeserved or overbearing.

> Family pressures are a massive thing. I spoke to a girl recently who was Arab and said she didn't like Arab men, but due to family pressures would have to marry an Arab man, and she felt she was willing to make that sacrifice. (Rahim, 22, helpline worker)

> A lot of young Muslims, their problems and issues are intertwined with their connections, their extended family and their immediate family, and you need to take each person's family in its own right. (Alina, 21, helpline worker)

One of the substantial issues, mentioned by both helpline workers and service providers we spoke to, regarded problems in the relationship between mothers-in-law and daughters-in-law. Overwhelmingly, such problems arose out of the amount of influence and control exerted by the mother-in-law over the daughter-in-law.

> A lot of people we get calls from, they tend to live with their in-laws anyway, so that in itself creates extra pressure: how to bring up the kids, how she should act, what she should do; she's not allowed to study, she's not allowed to go out, she's not allowed to do this, she's not allowed to do that. (Sana, 24, helpline worker)

Case study

Fahmida is a British woman from a Pakistani background in her early twenties who first called MYH when she was looking to move away out of her parental home. It became apparent that Fahmida had been beaten by her parents, and had suffered other forms of abuse, over a long period of time. She had hoped for many years that the abuse would stop as she became older. She now feels that only moving away will stop the abuse.

Fahmida contacted her support worker at university, and is currently receiving support from them, but she felt that she also needed support from someone who understood her cultural and faith background. She has found the idea of moving out of home difficult as she is afraid she may be ostracised from her family and community as a result.

MYH has provided a listening ear to Fahmida, as well as a safe space where she is able to discuss her options with those who will understand the aspects of her problems related to her faith and cultural background, without fear of being either judged or misunderstood.

The mediation service provider also mentioned this as a prominent concern:

> A lot of disputes are between husband and wife, marital disputes. Secondly to that, we have inter-generational issues – between mother-in-laws and daughter-in-laws, issues like that, or in relation to parents and children, and communication breakdowns between them.
> (Sana, 24, helpline worker)

The two GPs we interviewed both highlighted this problem, which they said could happen particularly when young British men married women from South Asia who then came to live in the UK. These women can be especially vulnerable because they lack a support network in Britain outside of their new family, and without speaking English it can be difficult for them to access services.

> The biggest one I have, that I see most often, is this issue with mothers-in-law abusing daughters-in-law. I mean, I'd say that in Tower Hamlets it's a huge problem, and it's one that's very hidden, because the women concerned are quite vulnerable. The ones that I've seen – and I've seen quite a lot – the ones that have come to light have been that bad that they've been referred to vulnerable adult social services, and they've even been called domestic slaves.
> What tends to happen is that young women are brought over from Bangladesh, they don't speak the language of the country, they're totally separated from their family, they have no support network here. They come into a household where there's generally quite a dominant mother-in-law or brother-in-law, or husband, or sister-in-laws, and they're made to do all the

Fig. 7 - Family concerns as a percentage of total relationship enquiries, 2006 - 2010

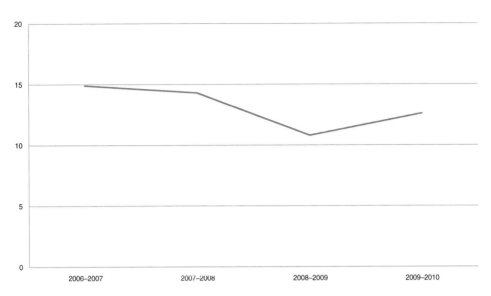

work in the house. And the way that they do it is that they don't let this person go out of the house so that they can't access anything. And even if they do go out, they don't speak the language, they don't know anything about the system of the country. **(Rukaiya, 33, GP in Tower Hamlets)**

A helpline worker also described a similar case:

We did have one woman, and she didn't have anyone here. She was living with her sister and her husband and they both used to beat her and she didn't know what to do. And basically, everyone else lived in Bangladesh and she never said anything to anyone because she was scared that they would taken her visa away, she wasn't that educated and wasn't really sure, so she never really told anyone. But they would really, really badly beat her. This other lady called on behalf of her, because she saw her wandering around in the street absolutely battered, she saw her and took her back to her place. **(Aaliyah, 25, helpline worker)**

Young women with these problems may only access primary care services when they have children and are obligated to bring their children for check-ups and vaccinations. At this point, they may be able to obtain help from their GP or via a referral to a specialist service.

You always have to talk to the mother about how they're feeling post-birth, explore their family situation, that's part of the assessment. And it tends to come out then, if at all. And sometimes it's something you pick up that's not quite right, and you can explore it further. But I think we see the tip of the iceberg. **(Rukaiya, 33, GP in Tower Hamlets)**

For many people, particularly members of Muslim communities, the role of the family in decision-making is well-known. Helpline workers reported service users having problems taking control of important decisions due to the strong influence of other family members, including those within the extended family.

> You don't just have the nuclear family that makes the decision, you've got the granddad and the grandma and the uncle and the aunt – and everybody seems to have an opinion. So your parents might agree, but then your extended family might not, and they can actually have quite a big say in what goes on in your life … Once you're 18 you can live your life as you wish, your parents have no influence … but we know that's not true. (Rahim, 22, helpline worker)

Overall, problems with family relationships are often a significant feature of the lives of young Muslims; mother-in-law and daughter-in-law relationships are a considerable issue, as are the nebulous family pressures over marriage, education, work and lifestyle choices.

Community

Community is a broad concept – on the helpline, it is not a separate category for calls, but this concept often came up in the interviews we conducted. The word was used to denote the network of Muslim families and friends which can influence a young person, especially if they live in areas where the Muslim population is proportionally quite high. This community is often a factor in their decision to call the helpline, though usually it is not the primary factor. This is because it can make a young person feel, in some situations, increased pressure to act in a particular way. Sometimes, for example, the disapproval of the wider community will not just affect a young person, but may also impact on other members of their family. If a young person makes a decision which is disapproved of by the wider community – in some cases, for example, divorce – their family can experience a loss of standing within the community, which can have a range of related effects. Many young people who call say that the community in which they live influences the decisions they make, sometimes including major decisions over marriage and careers.

> And even if you want to break out from your family, you know that your family will always be stigmatised in your community, so that's one of the reasons that hold you back. To say, if you want to get out and get married, then you think: 'You know what? There's gonna be repercussions for my sister, who's not going to have any proposals for what I've done; or my family, who are going to be stigmatised in the community.' So for every action you take there are a lot of repercussions, a lot of consequences … It's not clear cut, you need to think about many different aspects. (Alina, 21, helpline worker)

Family and community were also considered by focus group participants and helpline workers to be bigger factors in the decision-making of many young people than religion as an abstract idea.

> A lot of the time when you're talking about relationship problems, nothing much Islamic is mentioned. The only religious things that are mentioned are too blurred with cultural orientations that it's not really the big player. It tends to be 'my family, this is their tradition, they want this.' You won't hear someone quoting their personal religious beliefs and saying that

has an impact on my friendships or my relationships. (**Sana, 24, helpline worker**)

Also, the possibility of members of the community discovering information can discourage service access:

> There's a big issue of honour within the community, which can interfere with the use of external services. Obviously a helpline is one thing, where people don't have to know that you're calling the helpline or anything. But if you were to get people directly involved there's a family honour situation that can occur, and people are quite ashamed to do that. (**Rahim, 22, helpline worker**)

> If you're kind of getting people involved in your family, mediating and so on, it shows there's disharmony in the family. And I think one of the biggest issues with regard to relationships is this question of honour, and it's one of the reasons why we have so many calls with people having problems with their relationships and not being able to resolve them – because they don't want to upset anyone in the process. (**Farooq, 24, helpline worker**)

The effect of being forced into marriage can also be worsened for a young person by community gossip and pressure surrounding their marriage.

> Because not only is that girl or guy going through the trauma of being forced into marriage against their will, being taken back home [abroad], being brought back [to the UK] – but also the fact that the whole community knows. They're having pressure from the community, plus the extra added pressure from the family … who are like: 'Hold on, why are you getting divorced? It's only been a month. (**Aaliyah, 25, helpline worker**)

The young people focus group also described a community grapevine which could have detrimental effects on a young person. This might even prevent young people from confiding in their friends, for fear of being discovered:

> There's this idea that you have to absolutely hide it from your family, because your immediate family you can get in trouble with, but then there's extended family and the community finding out and so on. So even their generation of people they have to hide it from. (**Malika, 19, helpline worker**)

Previous research has confirmed that the community can play a major role in decisions for people from South Asian background (see, for example, Dwyer 2000). It is also supported by some anecdotal evidence, such as the Facebook group 'Asian aunties and uncles are like walking CCTVs !!' which has, at the time of writing, 17,000 members.

Sexual abuse

A numerically small but recurrent issue on the helpline is sexual abuse, including child sexual abuse: in most cases, the abuse has occurred in the past but the person remains psychologically affected.

> In the last few months, I've had a lot of cases of sexual abuse. We had one recently, where it was still ongoing. With other clients, it's happened, they're just trying to come to terms with it, and get over it. But it crosses that line as well, doesn't it? Sometimes, when it starts from an early age, they don't know what a relationship is – so they class it [the abuse] as a relationship. (**Aaliyah, 25, helpline worker**)

Sexual abuse is obviously not confined to any particular social group; and strong familial bonds can, in some cases, help in noticing early signs of abuse. In other cases, however, such bonds can exacerbate the abuse by discouraging the victim from seeking help, even later in life. This is linked to the broader issues of family and community; in some contexts, both can discourage a young person from seeking help. Cases on the helpline do include instances where the sexual abuse of a child by an older member of the family has been suppressed so as to avoid bringing the family into disrepute, even at the expense of the child's own well-being.

Sexuality

Concern over sexuality is a separate category on ELS, and a consistent issue. Helpline workers suggest that this is a particular concern for male callers.

> For example, with young boys, if we're talking about confusion surrounding sexual relationships, we tend to get a lot of males calling about homosexual feelings – in my experience I can't remember any females calling about similar feelings. Because there's no other service which can deal with this. (**Alina, 21, helpline worker**)

Often, these callers will not have approached another service, such as their GP, with concerns over sexuality. This may be due to a sense of embarrassment in discussing sexuality in person, rather than over the phone, as well as an expectation that a GP would not be able to provide advice or assistance on these issues. A GP we spoke to said that in cases where concern over sexuality was affecting mental health, he would refer the patient to a primary care psychologist, and while access to primary care psychologists has become easier than it has been in the past, it would nevertheless be difficult to obtain a referral to a psychologist trained specifically on sexuality-related issues. Psychologists trained in both sexuality and faith and cultural sensitivity are rarer still.

> There are psychosexual counsellors but they are very, very few and far between. And I think if you were to refer, it would be months and months before [the patient] would get any contact from them. (**Masood, 27, GP in Hackney**)

Dealing with problems

During the focus groups, young people and service providers were asked about working with young Muslims on the concerns highlighted in this report. Their responses were often similar and reflected some of the existing work on the topic. Key points included: the importance of understanding the relevance of faith, culture, family and community; the avoidance of stereotyping, and an awareness of the multitude of influences which can affect the decisions of a young person. Muslim mediation services were consistently suggested, in a range of focus groups and interviews, as particularly useful in improving service provision for young people.

General providers

Faith and cultural sensitivity

As in Malik et al. (2007), faith and cultural sensitivity was emphasised by the participants of this research as one of the most significant areas for improvement in mainstream services. Most participants thought that a basic understanding of faith principles was important for all those who work with young people from Muslim communities. Usually, however, the participants would emphasise that an abstract understanding is not sufficient – service providers should try to understand how faith, culture and society interact in creating the framework within which choices are made for individual people.

> The key is faith and cultural sensitivity ... Although we don't give *fatwas* [religious opinions] or direct our clients Islamically in any way, when they mention the Qur'an or a verse or *hadith* [saying of the Prophet], there's an implicit understanding that: 'I'm being understood here. If I go somewhere else, they won't really get where I'm coming from.' Although we work within the same parameters and principles as any general mediation service – we have the same training, all our volunteers are trained on conflict management and mediation skills, etc. But there's that thread running through about faith and cultural sensitivity. **(Co-founder, Muslim Mediation Service)**

Helpline workers pointed out that service users with relationship problems may not, and commonly do not, emphasise their faith as a primary factor. This was often seen to demonstrate the key role that 'culture' plays, particularly South Asian culture, with regard to family and community relationships and marriage.

> Not a lot of people who call about relationships have much regard for religion – they don't usually question whether it's wrong – maybe they just like the fact that we know their background. **(Alina, 21, helpline worker)**

When they talk, they talk about what's going on in the relationship, it doesn't tend to be about religion. (Sana, 24, helpline worker)

You'd be surprised, I've had some calls from Hindu people. They might see this as more of an 'Asian' helpline, in the sense that you've got cultural sensitivity, so when they're talking about caste systems and so on, you're more likely to understand where they're coming from – it's having that common background. (Farooq, 24, helpline worker)

Helpline workers, GPs, and others emphasised that service providers should be sensitive to these cultural influences without essentialising them. The cultural influences affecting two young people, even from the same faith group, may of course be entirely different, indicating the importance of understanding the individual perspective of a young person before giving advice. At the same time, there were areas where it was thought that providers should recognise potential cultural differences – particularly with regard to the role of the family and the community – and take care not to impose their own values (or what they may perceive to be the dominant social values) on a young person. The overall consensus was that service providers should be aware of the range of possible cultural attitudes on specific issues, but that such an awareness should only provide the basis for a full and personal exploration of the circumstances of an individual.

A number of helpline workers emphasised sensitivity with regard to living situations, such as in cases of marital problems or difficulties with in-laws. They felt that mainstream service providers could be too quick to suggest individualist remedies, such as separation, which may not be appropriate in every situation. It was suggested there were a number of ways to improve. For example, instead of asking: 'Why don't you move out of home?', the provider could ask: 'How would you/your parents feel about you moving out of home?'

I think it's just recognising the fact that there are cultural differences with someone from an Asian background, and that culture and tradition is very important to them. So for example, if someone's got problems at home, you can't just say to them: 'Why don't you move out?' There's a lot of stigma attached to a young girl moving out of home for no reason, or maybe living out at university. There's a lot of strings attached, there's a lot of stigma in the community. If someone says, my daughter's moved out, it's like: 'What do you mean, your daughter's moved out?' People need to just realise there's a lot of things to consider. (Aaliyah, 25, helpline worker)

For every action you take there are a lot of repercussions, a lot of consequences, which whoever is dealing with you needs to think about. It's not clear cut – you need to think about many different aspects. (Alina, 21, helpline worker)

So, for example, if the in-laws are elderly and the son has said: 'Ok, I'm going to look after them' – that makes it a lot more difficult for you to provide [his wife] with the option of moving out ... [You need to be] sensitive to it and say: 'Actually, in-laws play a very important part in your life.' You can't just say [to your in-laws]: 'I'm sorry, I don't like you,' and just move out. It's more recognising that; recognising who's got the influence to try and help them out of it.

You can utilise their own resources and their own support network in trying them to sort out their own issues, it's that kind of recognition of who plays what in this person's life, how influential they are and what their support network is, because you can try and utilise that. Don't assume anything. (Sana, 24, helpline worker)

Helpline workers also suggested that young Muslims, such as those from South Asian backgrounds, may be less inclined to disregard the opinions of their parents than young people from other communities. This suggests that providers should be aware of a range of methods for dealing with problems in the family.

I think some, not even non-Muslim, but non-Asian, people – they don't understand, sometimes, the attachment between the children and the parent … There's that respect and stuff. I think a lot of other people may be like: 'Hold on, if your parents say that to you, you can just say no,' and that might be limiting when it comes to the fact of the forced marriages thing. They may not fully comprehend how it started, why it started and the deeper implications. Because if – let's say a person has been forced into marriage, they've went and got married and came back. If this person does want to get separated from their partner and they go to a non-Muslim or non-Asian counsellor, that counsellor may not be aware of the cultural and community implications … It's that added pressure and, you know, just extra pain by other people that other people like non-Muslims and non-Asians might not be aware of. (Farooq, 24, helpline worker)

Knowledge and understanding of Muslim communities

Linked to the sensitivity around culture and faith was the suggestion that providers should make themselves aware of the basic tenets of the Muslim faith, as well as the ceremonies and traditions of the communities with whom they are working. Of course, an abstract understanding will not compensate for the experience that is gained from working closely with people. Nevertheless, it was felt that some basic knowledge would be useful for providers to have, while taking care to avoid the assumption that every young person experiences culture or religion in the same way.

And I think knowledge, [such as] in Islam you need to respect your elders. (Rahim, 22, helpline worker)

Trying to read up and really look up and have a good understanding of Islamic and Muslim cultures and Asian communities. As long as people have cultural and faith awareness, you can work and deal with any client of any faith and give support in a non-judgemental way. The key thing is that a client needs to feel they are understood. That the therapist or practitioner dealing with them doesn't think they're weird, or doesn't get them … (Co-founder, Muslim Mediation Service)

It's more knowledge that these people lack… just asking simple questions: 'How would your family feel about that? Could we work towards it? Maybe we could mediate between them [and you]?' **(Aaliyah, 25, helpline worker)**

It's just having a basic knowledge. For example, if you were sitting there talking to someone about boy/girl concern, and you're saying: 'So what you've got a girlfriend?' Well, actually, no, because in Islam you're not supposed to have a relationship [unless it is] a relationship when you're trying to get to know someone for marriage with the intention of marriage. You can't have sex before marriage. I know that amongst the major religions that is the same, but then that's seen more as something more historical than [something] people [actually] practice ... It's having that knowledge of recognising the ways they can deal with and realising why their family aren't happy, so again it goes back to knowing the boundaries you have as a person, knowing that extended family do play a part and it's important to know about the family and friends. **(Rahim, 22, helpline worker)**

Avoiding stereotypes and treating people as individuals

Along with knowledge and sensitivity on questions of faith and culture, service providers, especially helpline workers, emphasised the negative role that stereotyping can play in service provision. In particular, participants criticised common stereotypes, such as an exaggerated notion that young Asian women lack freedom and have all choices made for them by male members of their family. Stereotyping of this nature is well documented in academic research – see especially Dwyer (2000), who notes that: 'Gendered, classed, and racialised explanations reinforce a dominant representation of young Muslim women as both oppressed and powerless.' (See also: Brah and Minhas 1985; and Puar 1994, for more on this topic).

If you're talking about the whole marriage thing, and somebody happens to mention 'my parents are thinking about getting me married', [the service provider] will think automatically that the person is going to be forced into marriage. **(Alina, 21, helpline worker)**

When people see you they make assumptions about you. When people see you with a long beard they think: 'Oh my god, extremist!' when you could be a gentle soul, or when they see you as a hijabi who happens to be married, they just assume forced marriage or arranged married and you didn't choose. **(Sana, 24, helpline worker)**

The key to avoiding stereotypes, and to putting into practice a knowledge and understanding of Muslim communities, is to understand that service users are individuals; and to be aware that, within the context of a scarcity of time and resources, service providers are sometimes at risk of falling back on received ideas, methods and stereotypes. In interviews, the emphasis here was on the need to spend time exploring the individual situation of a service user.

You need to explore more, you need to explore where everything has come from. Yeah, they've got this issue, but that issue's arisen because of X,Y and Z. So you just need to explore everything; that's why you can have such long conversations with clients, and you don't get anywhere at the end of it because you're just getting the facts. Because you might have been on the phone for an hour and right at the end you'll probably get somewhere, and think: 'Ok, this is where it's probably stemmed from'. You kind of need to explore it a bit more. **(Malika, 19, helpline worker)**

It really depends on the situation, it's pretty individual to the person, to the family to where they're being brought up, it depends if it's a predominantly Muslim community or not and yeah it depends on what kind of relationship problems are in the family, with their siblings, with their friends. **(Alina, 21, helpline worker)**

Helpline workers made it clear that treating people as individuals does not mean disregarding their families, communities or cultures; rather, it means understanding how a particular individual sees themselves within this context. A young person living in St Albans, for example, might not feel the same connection with (or pressure from) the 'community' that a young person living in Tower Hamlets could experience. The levels of family influence, religiosity, and cultural influence will also vary depending on the individual; indeed, even for a single individual, such factors can vary substantially at different stages in their life.

You need to take each person's family in its own right. Because a lot of young Muslims, their problems and issues are intertwined with their connections, their extended family and their immediate family, and you need to take each person's family in its own right. So you need to explore that person's history in terms of their relationships, as a person, you can't generalise. You could have someone who has very, very little religious practices on a daily basis that impact them, to someone who has a lot, and that's so vast that you have to take them in their own right. **(Rahim, 22, helpline worker)**

Statutory providers

Statutory providers of services for young people include primary care surgeries and a range of linked services available depending on the nature of the concern.

Teachers could also be referred to as statutory providers where their role involves a measure of pastoral care for a young person. This section focuses on primary care surgeries, but includes advice relevant to other providers.

Providing language services

All the statutory providers we spoke to emphasised the importance of providing language services for recent immigrants who do not speak English as a first language. The providers' assessments of existing language service provision varied, ranging from 'very good' in certain boroughs, to 'adequate' or 'below adequate' in others.

The biggest problem is, [for those who don't] speak English, they can't access services unless there's interpreting or advocacy. So if you make that available to people they will access it ... So we [in Tower Hamlets] have English classes, ESOL, we have welfare and benefits advisors. Because a lot of people, the main issues that are impacting on their health is that they're poor, they're just struggling financially. If you can tell them in their own language, you can sit and explain to them: this is what you're entitled to. And also form-filling, so this is what we have for people in their own languages. Because a lot of people, they go to the job centre, they give them about 10 forms, and then they can't fill them in because they don't know how to write or read [in English.] ... There has to be some sort of education, otherwise all you see is children growing up in extreme poverty, overcrowding and poor stimulation, and that affects their health in later life. **(Rukaiya, 33, GP in Tower Hamlets)**

Whereas health advocates and interpreters did play a significant role in improving service access for non-English speakers, GPs still felt that there could be a gap in understanding between themselves and their patients and encouraged widening the access to English classes for recent immigrants.

Because of language more than anything else. I think the Muslims in this area are first generation, basically they're new arrivals of the first generation and they're very young. Other people who need a lot of access to healthcare are the older generation of Bengalis [and] they don't know how to go about it. When they come and see me as a GP, I can't even speak – I'm Guajarati – I can't even speak to them in Bengali or Urdu. They look at me really hopeful, they expect me to know it but I don't, and then they're very disappointed. And you can never quite get to the crux of what their problem is and it's frustrating for them, it's frustrating for you and you end up just trying to paper over the cracks. **(Masood, 27, GP in Hackney)**

Understanding the needs of women

Our research supported previous work which has shown that BME women in need of services can find accessing these services more difficult than men, for a variety of reasons. As with language services, provider views on the adequacy of service access varied: in some boroughs, it was felt to be 'very good'; in others, 'adequate' or 'less than adequate'. Some providers voiced concern over the ability of women from across different Muslim communities to access services. Some women, such as those from more religious backgrounds, may not feel comfortable with a male doctor, for example, and if a female doctor is not available they might even avoid going to the surgery altogether.

I used to work in West London, at Chelsea & Westminster Hospital, which ... has quite a large minority of Somali people. And there wasn't adequate provision for them. I think mainly in the fact that a lot of women will not talk to a man about this sort of stuff. Whereas ... in my [current] surgery we have a policy that there's always got to be one female doctor on, so women can always come and talk to someone if it's an emergency ... in other places they don't, you've got to have whoever's on. **(Rukaiya, 33, GP in Tower Hamlets)**

Understanding the needs of women was described as more than simply ensuring female doctors were available. With regard to women who were immigrants from South Asia or elsewhere, providers suggested that more could be done to encourage interaction, exercise and healthy lifestyles – for example, learning to cook in a healthier way, engaging in sports and fitness classes, and so on – which could significantly improve their health as well as the health of their families.

> You [should] also provide things that are female-friendly: women-only exercise, women-only English classes. (**Rukaiya, 33, GP in Tower Hamlets**)

GP services

The two GPs we spoke to, who practice in East London boroughs with proportionally high Muslim populations, understood the importance of their role as primary care providers who can often be the first point of contact for young people with relationship problems, particularly if the problem includes a medical dimension, such as pregnancy, contraception, abortion and domestic abuse. They both supported the continuation and expansion of specialist services (see 'Specialist services' below) which, they said, could ease the pressure on primary care. There was also a recognition of the limitations of dealing with major problems during short consultations.

> And remember, we have very little time, we have a 10 minute consultation with someone, and I think with a lot of the problems you might get coming to the helpline, 10 minutes is nowhere near enough to scratch the surface. You might need several sessions and it's very time consuming. In the middle of a busy doctor's surgery, I can understand why people with these kinds of problems would have difficulty seeing their GP. (**Masood, 27, GP in Hackney**)

There was some measured optimism about the future of provision for young people from Muslim communities. The GP who practiced in Hackney said he thought that the emerging group of young British Muslim doctors was likely to be a positive development. He suggested that this group is more likely to be able to identify with, and thus to provide better support to, their own generation.

> In the 1960s we had a large cohort of Indian and Pakistani doctors who ... I think could be quite unapproachable ... I think if I was 18 years old and had some kind of problem, family or home or whatever, I'd find it difficult to speak to someone of my dad's generation about it. But they're all retiring in the next 5-10 years, so it'll be a whole new batch of GPs – younger, better trained, better communication skills, more interested in holistic care. And I think things'll change, I think [young] people will feel more comfortable seeing their GP around more sensitive issues ... I think as the current generation become the service givers, they'll be better equipped to deal with it from that point of view. (**Masood, 27, GP in Hackney**)

With regard to training on faith and cultural sensitivity, the views of the GPs were generally similar: it was thought that although such training constituted a very small proportion of a medical degree, it may be unrealistic to expect more when considering the length and difficulty of the degree. Both doctors thought that it might be easier to institute post-qualification training for GPs who wish to learn more about the communities they will be working with. Examples were given of doctors who have committed themselves to learning about Muslim communities, South Asian languages, etc., in order to provide better and more holistic care; such examples could perhaps be recognised as cases of best practice. It was also suggested that this training could be standardised as a post-qualification certificate, though it was felt that such training should nevertheless remain voluntary.

> When you're in med school and you're learning so much other stuff, the last thing you want to hear is people talking to you about being sensitive to different faiths. You don't have time for it; it's right at the bottom of your list of priorities ... They probably could do more, but I don't think we'd really want any more. (Masood, 27, GP in Hackney)

Potential advantages

All the service providers we spoke to said that they supported the use of specialist services where needed, and that working as a Muslim with young people from Muslim communities could help a provider to connect and identify with the user. However, some providers also pointed out that there were advantages for someone perceived to be an 'outsider', particularly in areas of 'relationship' provision – such as sexual health – where young people might feel nervous about approaching a member of their own community.

> I mean, sometimes people feel more comfortable talking to someone outside their community, and they feel more embarrassed talking to someone within their community. And I found that especially when I worked in the sexual health in clinic in Whitechapel ... There's a lot of sexually transmitted infections, disease, but if you are a young Muslim Bengali man who thought he had an STD and went anonymously to the Whitechapel clinic, the last person you want to see is a female doctor with a name like mine, because you feel like you're being judged more than you would if you saw someone else. (Rukaiya, 33, GP in Tower Hamlets)

Specialist services

The need for specialist services focusing on Muslim communities in the UK was reiterated frequently in the focus groups as one of the key ways to deal with the relationship problems of young Muslims. GPs tended to be very strongly in favour of services like MYH, which, they said, provided a level of pastoral and emotional support that they as primary care providers simply did not have the resources or speciality to provide. There was also strong and consistent support from almost every interview and focus group for the increased use of Muslim mediation services as potentially transformative (see 'Mediation' below).

> In primary care, they're trying to shift more specialist work from secondary care, specialist clinics, back into primary care – which is putting a big strain on primary care work. Whereas before we might have referred diabetic patients to a specialist clinic, now they're being man-

aged purely in primary care. So the amount of work being taken on in primary care, every year it's getting more and more, so we always feel quite relieved when something specialist pops up and takes that burden away. (Masood, 27, GP in Hackney)

GPs also highlighted the fact that specialist services have long existed for other communities, and they have worked well in providing support to those communities. Young Muslims in particular have lacked the kind of support from their own community that has been available to other young people.

I think it's actually good to have a specialist service. Lots of other ethnic groups, lots of other communities, have a special service that's available to them. So I think it's actually good because GPs are meant to be generalists, you can't expect every one of them to have that same breadth of knowledge, or put their own prejudices aside to help a certain person from a different background. That's an ideal world, but I think it's really good to have a specialist service there. (Masood, 27, GP in Hackney)

I think it's a bad idea to try and get rid of specialist things like [MYH] ... There's a need for it, at least for the next 10 or 20 years. (Rukaiya, 33, GP in Tower Hamlets)

As described above, GPs suggested that many young people may feel more comfortable discussing issues with someone who they perceive will understand their cultural and faith background. Though providers can, and should, increase their own cultural and faith sensitivity, there may, nevertheless, be times when, for some people, the best support can be provided by a co-member of the community.

I think if you were a young Muslim and you wanted to go to your GP, and you got there and there was a stuffy old white bloke, you're just going to perceive that that person isn't going to understand the intricacies of why things are difficult. (Rukaiya, 33, GP in Tower Hamlets)

Listening

Listening services like MYH were highlighted by young people, helpline workers and GPs as important in helping young people deal with relationship problems, as outlined in detail in previous work on this topic (Malik et al. 2007). The nature of 'relationship' problems, which can often be nebulous and connected to a host of other issues, requires more in terms of provision than short consultations with a GP. Young people were asked about ways to improve provision in a focus group, and they suggested increasing the capacity of specialist services.

There needs to be a lot more organisations like MYH, because it's just getting ridiculous, I could tell you one hundred and one stories from my community, and things are getting really out of hand. I think it's really, really bad that there's not people out there helping young people. All the kind of organisations around me are more for dealing with the problems the elder community are having – how to convince your kids to do this and that. I think it's ridiculous that there's not more organisations like this, especially in areas like East London, Luton, Bradford. (Shaheen, 21)

Though existing statutory services like the Forced Marriage Unit were regarded as useful, they were generally seen as too focused on extreme cases to be useful to the majority of young people. Primary care and psychological services were seen in the same way – many young people facing relationship difficulties will not access such services until their problems are at a very advanced stage. The importance for young Muslims of being able to speak to their peers about problems with family, marriage, or relationships was emphasised.

> There are services, but they're too specific ... For example, someone who is to the point where they're literally afraid that a forced marriage is going to happen, yeah, there's a service for that – but that's extreme cases. Someone who sort of knows that their family might do that, verged on it, have been controlling them for quite a while, they need someone to talk to about how to build their relationships and maybe make their parents more aware of their understanding of who they are, and how they don't want that to be imposed on them. That person might not benefit from a service like Forced Marriage Unit. Because it's not at that extreme, it's not like you're going to call the police ... **(Malika, 19, helpline worker)**

Counselling

MYH workers refer many cases on to counselling services, including specialist counselling services, and they spoke in favour of improving both access to, and provision of, these services. As with listening above, the suggestion was that complex and multi-faceted problems often require a substantial amount of talking. Muslim counsellors use the same person-centred methods as other counsellors, but may be able to better identify with service users in some cases.

> But a lot of the new callers who want counselling, let's say if they've gone through something really traumatic in their childhood and they've realised they need to talk about it face to face, then they would prefer a Muslim counsellor to anybody else, just because the [counsellor] would recognise the cultural implications that would go with whatever they've experienced. **(Rahim, 22, helpline worker)**

There was a feeling amongst helpline workers that Muslim counsellors were particularly well-placed to help with the complexities of family and community that often accompany relationship problems for young British Muslims.

> So that's why if you have a Muslim counsellor at least they'll be aware of it and they can address that as well ... The Muslim counsellor would understand that more than anyone else. I think other problems, when it comes to stuff like self-harm or suicide, even abuse, it's not just that specific problem. This is what I've learnt since being on the service, I always thought it's just that specific problem you'd need help or counselling with, [but] it's the wider context as well and it usually is the result of the wider context ... It's not just your family or your friends, it's the community, your family back home, etc. etc. They are layers and I'm not sure if a non-Muslim counsellor may understand fully. **(Sana, 24, helpline worker)**

Factbox: Muslim Mediation Services

History

- Most local London councils have a neighbour mediation service, or a community mediation service, which provides services for everyone across the community.

- Newham has a community mediation service, Conflict & Change. Local imams and mosques became aware of Conflict & Change and felt that it was something with which Muslim communities needed to be more involved.

- A number of imams approached Canning Town Muslim Trust and said that an increasing number of families were going to the mosque with family problems, marital breakdowns, and parent/child issues. These imams felt they were often not equipped to deal with these problems, lacking the necessary skills and training.

- A baseline study was carried out by Canning Town Muslim Trust and Conflict & Change. This confirmed that there was significant demand for a specialist service. A successful project, part-funded and supported by Conflict & Change, was piloted for about a year.

- Following on from this, the Muslim Mediation Service was launched in 2003.

Aims of MMS

- To promote conflict-resolution based on the Islamic values of fostering unity, peace and understanding amongst Muslims and in the wider community, primarily in Newham.

- To provide the Muslim community with a mediation service towards resolving personal, familial, professional and community conflicts.

- To equip members of the Muslim community with the skills and capacity to manage their own personal, familial, professional and community conflicts.

- To enhance peace and understanding between the Muslim and wider community by working with other Muslim and non-Muslim organisations so as to bring together the Muslim and the wider communities.

Services

- Weekly drop-in sessions with an experienced Muslim family mediator, aimed primarily at those living in the London Boroughs of Newham, Redbridge, Waltham Forest, Barking & Dagenham, Hackney and Tower Hamlets.

Mediation

The need to expand and increase the use of Muslim mediation services was suggested time and again throughout the focus groups. The providers we spoke to saw social services as being too quick to break up families and insist on separation. It was generally agreed that mediation should, at least, be considered as possibly a better way of dealing with problems in marriage, or between parents and children, in the Muslim community than a social services intervention. GPs in particular said that many women were unwilling to go to social services, fearing that they would be ostracised from their family or lose custody of their children. Furthermore, it was felt that mediation could often work in setting boundaries, explaining problems to the people concerned, settling on solutions without necessarily splitting up families, and often resulting in better outcomes than other types of intervention.

> [Service users] often disengage with their service unless it's something they have specifically gone out to find out about. Because they don't want to rock the boat, they don't want to make things worse at home. And [providers] have actually found that sometimes when they intervene, it makes the situation much worse. They might take the woman out of the scenario for maybe a couple of months. She's staying in a hostel somewhere, ends up going back home, and it's worse than before. And now she doesn't want to get in contact with anyone. **(Masood, 27, GP in Hackney)**

> What you need to do is more kind of mediation, more talking to them, more talking to the husband, trying to set out certain boundaries, you agreeing with the husband on an action plan as opposed to you being separated. **(Malika, 19, helpline worker)**

> [We need] a taskforce which brings families together as opposed to tearing them apart, which is what happens. So if you've got a group that tries to resolve issues and tries to bring people together – we don't have enough mediation services and that's what we need. Especially with relationship issues, because that goes across the board between boy-girl concerns, marriages, friendships, relationships with families – trying to bring these people together and trying to create an understanding, more communication. **(Farooq, 24, helpline worker)**

GPs also suggested mediation as an important method for dealing with various problems they had encountered. In particular, difficult situations for women – particularly young immigrant women – were seen as not being improved by traditional social services intervention.

> I don't know what type of funding there is, or whether it's unreasonable to expect this, but it sounds like family mediation is something we could use in the community. Refuges and things like that are not the answer for these communities because they don't want to split their families up. For other people you could just say, if you're being abused you need to get out of that situation, and set up an independent life. But for these women, who don't speak English, don't have the right to work, they have children, it's not going to happen … So maybe some sort of mediation service, someone going into the family, who's sensitive, who speaks the language, to try and empower these women a bit more … **(Rukaiya, 33, GP in Tower Hamlets)**

Traditional intervention in such situations was seen by GPs as carrying a substantial risk of making the situation worse – and concomitantly making people less likely to approach services with the expectation of receiving help.

> The only way you can intervene is to go into the family situation. And the problem with that is that the woman doesn't want you to do that, because that's gonna make her life more difficult. Because if you go in, ultimately the family know that she's whistleblown. And she's not willing to leave, that's not the ultimate aim. So what you're doing is risking, first of all losing her trust, because she's come in and told you something and then you are gung ho going into her family situation. And secondly that her situation could be made worse by any intervention that you do. So this one is particularly difficult. This is where I think mediation needs to take place, to try and ... also to understand the reasons. **(Rukaiya, 33, GP in Tower Hamlets)**

A co-founder of the Muslim Mediation Service was interviewed for this research project. She agreed with many of the thoughts expressed by other providers and young people.

> Firstly, I think it's a great intervention because in relation to social services, and other interventions like that, in our communities those interventions are still taboo; there's still a fear that: 'Are our children going to be taken away? Oh, we don't want people to find out.'
>
> I feel that mediation is much more relevant and useful because it totally takes the Islamic approach: of people sitting down and consulting with each other, families coming together and trying to resolve problems together; it's a theme running through Qur'anic verses, when there is marital or family discord, families sitting down and talking through it. An arbitrator being set up, and getting everyone to talk. That's the value of mediation, it's the idea that people can come to a setting, feel like nobody's being judged or blame, but each party is being heard. And it's giving a chance to air their views, air their needs, air their concerns, and a trust is built. Everyone tries to understand what the situation is and what's going on. And the next stage takes them to – what has to happen now?
>
> I think it's an amazing process, because it really does help people talk things through. I find a lot of the time in the Muslim community, we don't have this trend, or even in the general community – this trend of 'let's talk it through.' It's usually: here's the problem, you're to blame, I'm not to blame, let's have a fight and get it over and done with. But mediation promotes this idea of people really trying to talk things through. And for the Muslim community, it's a real benefit because, for us, we're the only Muslim mediation service in the UK. A lot of clients come to us, rather than going to Relate or somewhere else, we have the cultural and faith sensitive approach. They feel safe, they feel it's ok, they can talk about this, they can talk about issues. **(Co-founder, Muslim Mediation Service)**

Improving mediation

Some of the key problems identified with existing mediation services were: a lack of funding and access, an overemphasis on older members of the community, and an under-representation of young people.

A lack of investment in mediation services has clearly restricted access: funding has not been as forthcoming as it could be from statutory bodies, charitable trusts, or the Muslim community itself. Government agencies, in particular, were seen as being more likely to fund projects which look impressive but are, in fact, short-term and low-impact.

> It's a massive problem of lack of funding … Mosques see the value in our work, but because of their own financial restraints are not willing to plough the money … It's reaching a really difficult time at the moment – we've got 3 members of staff, they're all part-time, there isn't that organisational capacity in place to fulfil the needs of however many Muslims like in the UK. We are stretched at capacity, our caseworker is seeing clients back-to-back, and now we are charging clients. Unfortunately we can't take some of these cases on because we can't afford it. (Co-founder, Muslim Mediation Service)

Current mediation provision was also criticised for being dominated by older members of the community to the exclusion of young people. This also meant that mediators were perceived as being more likely to judge in favour of parents than children. It was also suggested that mediation could be broadened to a community taskforce which, crucially, would represent young people as well as older people.

> It'd be great to have that medium where you can get together and have a task force where you can mediate between whatever's going on, or have monthly or weekly meetings and focus on a certain issue every month, and say how can we combat this, but make it open. (Malika, 19, helpline worker)

> A lot of the time with communities it'll only be the elders that are there and they'll be the only ones who are leading the meetings … It is a bit hard to open up, because that could be one of your relatives there or talking about maybe sexual abuse or just relationships in general and I think maybe it might be good to have a youth-led service where the youth can come in and talk. (Sana, 24, helpline worker)

> The majority of the time, these services are focused on older adults and married couples and families, and they're less likely to advocate the voice of a younger child, or the types of individuals that call us. (Farooq, 24, helpline worker)

> Maybe because they're run by an older generation, it doesn't reflect our generation. (Imran, 19)

Some helpline workers also said that mediation services – perhaps mainstream ones – could use an adaptive approach when working with Muslim families, taking into account what can often be strong family bonds and an unwillingness to split apart. Some also suggested that awareness of mediation, including informal mediation via family or friends, could be improved.

> But it's also to do with the approach. Even within our generation, a lot of youth still define themselves by the relationships that they have ... Mediation services need to have a different approach when it comes to Muslim families. They need to have more of a collectivist approach, and less focus on identifying problems with individuals, but more with the family unit. (Malika, 19, helpline worker)

> I think the problem more is that people aren't willing to go out of their way to find people to mediate – they can find people amongst their own family and friends who can help too. (Sana, 24, helpline worker)

Conclusion

This report marks the first in a series of research projects being undertaken to look at ways of improving services for young people from Muslim communities. After many years of conceptualising new and progressive ways of providing services, pioneered by a range of organisations and scholars, new research like this is aimed to directly feed into the way services are delivered.

MYH was set up in 2001 to ensure that young people from a Muslim faith background did not have to suffer alone and in silence. Since then, MYH has helped over 28,000 young British Muslims lift themselves out of despair. However, young British Muslims still need help – most indicators show that their levels of social exclusion remain the same, if not worse. Unfortunately, it appears that service provision is patchy, and as a result services often still struggle to meet the needs of individuals from the young British Muslim communities.

This report highlights the need for more support services like those provided by MYH, but also demonstrates how essential it is for mainstream and statutory agencies to develop the capacity to provide faith and culturally sensitive support to Muslim youth in the UK. The report also clearly demonstrates that to overcome the challenges they face, community engagement for the sake of engagement is a powerful tool when seeking to help young people from ethnic communities that experience high levels of disadvantage and deprivation, and who are more than likely to be discriminated against compared to their counterparts and other ethnic minority groups.

Faith and cultural sensitivity is outlined in this report as a series of basic guidelines, many of which will already be familiar to service providers, though perhaps not systematically applied. While it is crucial that providers working with Muslim communities understand both the principles of the religion and the specific cultural backgrounds of those with whom they are working, it is even more important that sensitivity does not stop there. This is because theoretical knowledge, without understanding how faith and culture matter in the lives of specific people, can actually be damaging by leading to stereotyping: Muslim women wearing headscarves as devoutly religious, for example, or Asian young people as subject to repressive households or automatically as members of large extended families. A significant barrier to service provision as described by both service providers and service users in this report was precisely the idea – whether real or perceived – that they would not be understood as individuals, but would be essentialised into broad racial or religious categories.

If young British Muslims are reluctant to access support from the mainstream for fear of being misunderstood, the results are likely to be experiences of further isolation and marginalisation. Thus, meaningful engagement and support – which is faith and culturally sensitive – can be empowering and transformative, helping young British Muslims to overcome barriers to social inclusion and have better access to the services and ultimately opportunities that promote good psychological and emotional wellbeing.

Bibliography

Abbas, T. (2005) *Muslim Britain: Communities Under Pressure*. London: Zed Books.

Ahmad, F. (2001). Modern Traditions? British Muslim Women and Academic Achievement. Gender and Education, 13(2), 137 – 152.

Ahmed, S. (2008) Seen and Not Heard, Voices of Young British Muslims. Leicester: Policy Research Centre.

Ansari, H. (2003) Muslims in Britain. London: Minority Rights Group International.

Archer, L. (2001). 'Muslim Brothers, Black Lads, Traditional Asians': British Muslim Young Men's Constructions of Race, Religion and Masculinity in *Feminism & Psychology*, 11(1), 79-105.

Archer, L. (2002). 'Change, culture and tradition: British Muslim pupils talk about Muslim girls' post-16 "choices"' in *Race, Ethnicity & Education*, 5(4), 359-376.

Ballard, R., ed. (1994) *Desh Pardesh: The South Asian Presence in Britain*. London: Hurst.

Basit, T. (1997) *Eastern Values, Western Milieu: Identities and Aspirations of Adolescent British Muslim Girls*. Aldershot: Ashgate.

Bhugra, G. and Bhui, K. (1999) 'Racism in psychiatry: paradigm lost-paradigm regained' in *International Review of Psychiatry*, 11(2-3), 236-243.

Bhui, K. (2010) 'Culture, religion and health care' in International Journal of Integrated Care (21) Jan-Mar 2010, available at: http://www.ncbi.nlm.nih.gov/pmc/articles/PMC2834912/

Brah, A., and Minhas, R. (1985), 'Structural racism or cultural difference? Schooling for Asian girls', in Gaby Weiner (ed.) *Just a Bunch of Girls*. London: Open University Press.

Brah, A. (1987) Women of South Asian origin in Britain: issues and concerns in *South Asia Research* (7).

Breger, R., and Hill, R. (1998) *Cross-Cultural Marriage: Identity and Choice*. London: Berg.

Burman, E., and Chantler, K. (2005) 'Domestic violence and minoritisation: Legal and policy barriers facing minoritized women leaving violent relationships' in *International Journal of Law and Psychiatry* (28/1) 59-74.

Charsley, K., and Shaw, A. (2006), 'Introduction: South Asian transnational marriages in comparative perspective.' Special issue on 'South Asian Transnational Marriages' in Global Networks 6(4), 331-344.

DCLG and the Change Institute (2008) *Understanding Muslim Ethnic Communities*.

Dwyer, C. (2000) Negotiating Diasporic Identities: Young British South Asian Muslim Women in *Women's Studies International Forum*, 23(4), 475–486.

Fulat, S. & Jaffrey, R. (2006) 'Muslim Youth Helpline: A Model of Youth Engagement in Service Delivery' in *Youth and Policy,* (92), 151-171

Gangoli, G. et al. (2006) *Forced Marriage and Domestic Violence among South Asian Communities in North East England.* Bristol: School for Policy Studies.
Available at: http://www.nr-foundation.org.uk/downloads/ForcedMarriage_report.pdf

Greater London Authority (2006) *Muslims in London.*
Available at: http://www.iengage.org.uk/images/stories/muslimsinlondon.pdf

Hall, Stuart (1992) 'The question of cultural identity' in Stuart Hall, David Held, & Tom McGrew (Eds.), *Modernity and its Future* (pp. 273–325). Cambridge: Polity.

Home Office (2000) *A Choice by Right.* Available at: http://www.fco.gov.uk/resources/en/pdf/pdf14/fco_choicebyright2000

Home Office Forced Marriage Unit (2010) *Updated statistics - email correspondence 02/03/10.*

Kleinman, A. (1988) *The Illness Narrative. Suffering, Healing & the Human Condition.* New York: Basic Books

Lynch, J.; Smith, G.; Kaplan, G.; and House, J. (2000) 'Income inequality and mortality: importance to health of individual income, psychosocial environment, or material conditions' in *British Medical Journal,* April 29, 320(7243), 1200–1204.

Malik, R. (2006) 'British or Muslim: Creating a Context for Dialogue' in *Youth and Policy* (92), 91-105.

Malik, R.; Shaikh, A.; and Suleyman, M. (2007) *Providing Faith and Culturally Sensitive Support Services to Young British Muslims.* London: National Youth Agency.

Mogra, I. (2006) 'Intervention for Transformation: Activities among Young Muslims of Britain' in *Youth and Policy* (92), 133-149

Nazroo, J.Y. (1997) Ethnicity and Mental Health. Policy Studies Institute: London.

Roberts, J. (2006) 'Making a place for Muslim Youth Work in British Youth Work' in *Youth and Policy* (92), 19-31

Tyrer, D. and Ahmad, F. (2006) *Muslim Women and Higher Education: Identities, Experiences and Prospects.* Liverpool: Liverpool John Moores University.
Available at: http://www.aulaintercultural.org/IMG/pdf/muslimwomen.pdf

Verma, G., Zec, P. and Skinner, G. (1994) *The Ethnic Crucible: Harmony and Hostility in Multi-Ethnic Schools.* London: Falmer Press.

Wellock, V. (2008) 'Domestic abuse: Black and minority-ethnic women's perspectives' in *Midwifery* 26(2), 181-188.

...ung Muslim Voices (2008/9) *Project Report.* Available at: http://www.irr.org.uk/pdf/YMV_report.pdf